Choices

Donna Lewis

Doris Rapp

William R. Parks

Stanwrite@aol.com

www.wrparks.com

This book is dedicated to Julie Billings who took the first step and to Bill Parks for making the rest possible.

CHOICES

Once upon a time
When time was new,
Someone said all birds were white;
There was no color or hue.

All the birds were called
To come and use
Any color he or she
Might choose.

Paint pots of yellow, blue,
Brown, black or red,
A single color or perhaps
Speckled instead.

One bird chose black
And black it became,
It looked in a mirror
With a plain wooden frame.

It frowned. That's not
What I want to be.
Can you please put
A spot of color on me?

A bright red splash
On top of each wing
With a strip of white gold
Was just the thing.

A red-winged blackbird
He became.

A loud, squawking jay
Called, "Hey! Hey! Hey!
"Bright blue for me
With a touch of gray.
"I'll be a beautiful,
Flashy, happy Blue Jay."

The Blue Jay perched
In a nearby pine tree.
"Don't you think
I'm the prettiest bird
You will ever see?"

A small finch
Slipped and rolled
In spilled yellow paint.
"Help, oh, help, " he screeched
I'm going to faint!"

You will be fine.
We will add some black
Here and there.
What beauty you'll bring
As you fly through the air!

One early bird sang,
 I want a colorful vest
Mix yellow with red
To make me a Robin Redbreast.

Everyone will be happy
To hear the songs I sing,
To see my bright color
As the first sign of spring.

A meadow lark just couldn't
Make up her mind.
She looked in every paint
Pot she could find.

Perhaps some warm brown
Feathers on my top
With speckles and sprinkles
That show when I hop?

I will sit on a
Fence post and sing
A joyful song
To make everyone happy
All day long.

Mr. Cardinal then
Spoke up and said,
"Scarlet for me, please,
"With a topknot
"On my head."

Mrs. Cardinal chirped,
"I like red, but for me
A bit subdued.
Can you make my color
Softer hued?"

A larger bird came next,
Aggressive and proud,
A woodpecker who is
Always noisy and loud.

"I want to be seen,
As well as heard.
Make me a bright-looking
Noticeable bird."

"Everyone looks when I
Peck a hole for a nest.
I want colors that will
Show my flashiest best."

Two smaller birds
Were waiting in line.
The sparrow chirped,
"Brown will be fine.

Make my colors
To blend with the tree.
Mixed grays and browns
Will be right for me."

The lady wren turned her head
From side to side,
This way and that
With eyes opened wide.

"No red for me, no yellow,
Nothing bright.
Different browns will help me
Stay out of sight."

Another happy bird came
With a hop and a jump.
He was perky and trim
And pleasingly plump.

"No brown for me," he chirped.
"Can you paint me bright blue?
I want to be seen,
With a colorful breast, too."

"Imagine the colors,
Can't you just see
What a beautiful bird
I am going to be!"

The dove arrived late,
You know they are slow,
The paint's almost gone;
But wait! You know what artists say.

A little of this, a smidgeon
Of that will make a nice gray.
"Oh, yes," cooed the dove,
And wandered happily away.

And so, day after day,
Hundreds of birds came;
Day after day,
No two kinds the same.

Of course, you know
This tale is not true,
But I like to pretend,
I hope you do, too.

Woodpecker

Bluebird

Wren

Sparrow

Bluejay

Meadowlark

Robin

Dove

Goldfinch

Cardinal
(male)

Cardinal
(female)

Red-winged
Blackbird

Acknowledgments

Cover photo, title page photo and pages 1, 2, 3, 4, 6, 7, 9, 10, 14, 15, 16, 17, 18, 19, 21, 22 photos Copyright © Doris Rapp

Pages 5, 8, 12, 13, & 20 photos Copyright © Julie Billings

Page 11 photo Copyright © Kevin Cole

www.ingramcontent.com/pod-product-compliance
Lightning Source LLC
Chambersburg PA
CBHW060819290526
45792CB00005BB/1726